Signature Tastes®

www.SignatureTastes.com

Do you remember that place your sister took us to when we stayed with her last year?

Why yes. Yes we do.

Those restaurant recipes and a whole lot more. We all remember a great meal...

the *company*, the *place* and the *food.*

About the Author

Steven W. Siler is a firefighter-cum-chef serving in Charleston, South Carolina. He is the author of several cookbooks of restaurant recipes from across the nation.In addition, he has served as an editor and contributing writer for several food publications.

Take your tastebuds for a stroll through Charleston's *Signature* restaurants!

www.CharlestonCulinaryTours.com
(843) 259-2966

Shellfish A La Nicoise
39 Rue de Jean
39 John St., Charleston

Roasted Garlic:
8 bulbs garlic
vegetable oil
Shrimp & Scallops a la Nicoise:
¼ C. heavy cream
1 tsp parmesan cheese
5 diver scallops
5 shrimp 26/30 or larger, peeled &
deveined

6 oz. penne pasta, cooked
3 oz. roasted garlic
½ bag thin green beans, blanched &
finely chopped
4 nicoise olives
¼ C. sun dried tomatoes, chopped
2 oz. vegetable oil
kosher salt for seasoning

Roasted Garlic:

1. Place garlic in baking dish or sauté pan. Cover in vegetable oil and roast in the oven at 425°F for 15 minutes.

2. Once mixture is done, remove the garlic bulbs, place in food processor or blender and blend until the mixture becomes smooth.

Shrimp & Scallops a la Nicoise:

1. In a large sauté pan, add vegetable oil and sear scallops and shrimp. Season with kosher salt.

2. Once the scallops and shrimp have a nice light brown color, flip and add pasta, tomatoes, olives and green beans.

3. Add the roasted garlic puree followed by the cream and reduce to a thick Alfredo consistency. Finish with some fresh parmesan cheese.

Philip Simmons (June 9, 1912 – June 22, 2009) was an American artisan and blacksmith specializing in the craft of ironwork. Simmons spent 78 years as a blacksmith, focusing on decorative iron work, including the Heart Gate above.

BBQ Shrimp & Grits
82 Queen
82 Queen St., Charleston

For Lowcountry Grits:
1 C. heavy cream
¼ lb butter
1 qt water
2 C. quick grits
salt & pepper, to taste
For Southern Comfort BBQ Sauce:
¼ lb bacon, diced
½ C. red onion, diced

½ C. red bell pepper, diced
½ C. green bell pepper, diced
2 14 oz Heinz® ketchup
½ C. brown sugar
3-4 Tbsp Southern Comfort®
salt & pepper, to taste
For Shrimp:
2 lb shrimp

For Lowcountry Grits:

1. Heat cream and water to a boil. Add butter, salt, and pepper. Slowly add grits and reduce heat.

2. Cook for 20 minutes, being careful not to scorch mixture, stirring constantly.

For Southern Comfort BBQ Sauce:

1. Cook bacon until almost done. Add onions and peppers, and sauté until done.

2. Flame with Southern Comfort®. Add all the remaining ingredients.

3. Simmer for 10 minutes, then cool. Sauce will last under refrigeration for several weeks.

For Shrimp:

1. Sauté, poach, or grill the shrimp.

2. Place the shrimp in the Southern Comfort® bbq sauce and simmer for 1 minute.

Succotash with Shrimp
Acme Lowcountry Kitchen
31 J C Long Blvd, Isle of Palms

For Succotash
1/2 C. speckled butterbeans, drained
1/2 C. field peas
3/4 C. whole kernal corn
6 diced snow peas
3 slices bacon, chopped

2 Tbsp heavy cream
1 tsp garlic, diced
1/2 tsp tarragon
(10) 21-25 shrimp, peeled and sauteed
salt & pepper, to taste

1. Fry the bacon in a saute pan for 5-7 minutes, until fat renders out and bacon starts to crisp.

2. Add remaining vegetables, and continue sauteing for another 2-3 minutes until almost tender.

3. Add heavy cream, tarragon and garlic, and simmer for another 1-2 minutes.

4. Add sauteed shrimp on top. Salt and pepper to taste and serve.

Shrimp and Grits
Amen Street Raw Bar
Charleston, South Carolina

1/2 C. tasso ham (ground in a food processor)

2 Tbsp green onions, sliced thin

3/4 C. heavy cream

1 batch roasted tomato puree (recipe below)

12 large shrimp

Stone ground grits (recipe below)

Roasted Tomato Puree:

3 vine ripened tomatoes, cut into wedges

1 Tbsp garlic, minced

2 Tbsp shallots, sliced thin

4 Tbsp red wine vinegar

3 Tbsp molasses

Grits:

4 C. water

1/2 C. cream

3 Tbsp butter

salt and pepper to taste

1 C. stone ground grits

1. For the tomato puree, place tomatoes on a baking rack and season with salt and pepper. Roast in a 500-degree oven for 20 minutes. Let rest to room temperature and remove skin and seeds. Roughly chop. In a saucepan, place the garlic and shallots with 2 tablespoons of olive oil and saute for 2 minutes. Add tomatoes, vinegar and molasses and turn heat to medium. Cook, stirring constantly, until most of the liquid has evaporated and set aside.

2. Bring water and butter to a boil, slowly whisking in grits. Turn heat to low and cook 20 minutes, stirring to prevent sticking. Whisk in cream and let rest 10 minutes before serving.

3. To prepare, place a large saute skillet on a burner over medium-high heat. Once the pan is warm, addd 2 tablespoons of olive oil. Then add shrimp. Saute 1 minute on each side. Add tasso and tomato puree, and pour over grits to serve. Serves two.

Carolina Gold Rice
Anson Mills
Available throughout Charleston

6 cups spring or filtered water

Fine sea salt

1 C. Anson Mills Carolina Gold Rice

2 to 3 Tbsp unsalted butter, cut into small pieces

½ teaspoon freshly ground black pepper

1. Adjust an oven rack to the middle position and heat the oven to 300 degrees. Line a rimmed baking sheet with parchment paper.

2. In a heavy-bottomed 3½-quart saucepan, bring the water and 1 tablespoon of salt to a boil over high heat. Add the rice, stir once, and as soon as the water returns to a boil, reduce the heat to low.

3. Simmer gently, uncovered, stirring occasionally, until the rice is just tender with no hard starch at its center, about 15 minutes.

4. Drain the rice in a fine-holed footed colander and rinse well with cool water. Shake the colander to drain off excess water.

5. Evenly distribute the rice the prepared baking sheet. Place the baking sheet in the oven and allow the rice to dry for about 5 minutes, gently turning the grains from time to time with a spatula.

6. Dot with the butter and sprinkle with the pepper and salt to taste. Return the baking sheet to the oven and allow the rice to warm through, occasionally turning the grains, until the butter has melted and the rice is hot, about 5 minutes more. Transfer to a warmed serving bowl and serve immediately.

Pralines and Praline Butter
A.W. Shuck's
70 State St., Charleston

(1) 3" praline, chopped fine
¼ cup sugar
1 Tbsp cinnamon
1 lb butter, softened
1 tsp vanilla

Pralines:
2 cups granulated sugar
1 cups whipping cream
1/3 stick butter
1 ½ C. whole pecans

Pralines:

1. Combine all ingredients except the pecans in a heavy saucepan. Over medium heat stir mixture until it comes to a boil.

2. Turn heat down to medium-low and continue to stir. Cook until mixture reaches 238 to 241 degrees F on a candy thermometer or soft ball stage.

3. Stir in the pecans. Remove from heat. Stir until the mixture begins to thicken and becomes creamy and cloudy.

4. Drop onto parchment paper, buttered pan or buttered marble slab, using a spoon or ice cream scoop. Let cool.

Praline Butter:

1. Mix all ingredients together well. Roll in parchment paper and freeze.

2. Cut into slices and on top of sweet potato pancakes.

Macaroni and Cheese
Bertha's Kitchen
2332 Meeting Street Rd., Charleston

Kosher salt, plus more to taste
1 lb. elbow macaroni
4 tbsp. unsalted butter
¼ cup flour
3 cups milk
1½ lb. (6 cups) grated sharp white

cheddar
Freshly ground black pepper and cayenne, to taste
8 oz. (2 cups) grated sharp regular cheddar

1. Heat oven to 375°.

2. Bring a large pot of salted water to a boil and add pasta; cook, stirring, until cooked halfway through, about 3-minutes. Drain pasta and set aside.

3. Heat butter in a 2-qt. saucepan over medium-high heat. Whisk in flour and cook until smooth, about 1 minute.

4. Add milk and cook, whisking, until sauce is thickened and coats the back of a spoon, about 10 minutes.

5. Add white cheddar and stir until melted and smooth; season with salt, pepper, and cayenne.

6. Stir in pasta and transfer to a 9″ x 13″ baking dish; cover top evenly with regular cheddar and bake until bubbly and top is golden brown, about 35 minutes.

7. Let cool for 10 minutes before serving.

Boston Butt BBQ Basting Sauce
Bessinger's
1602 Savannah Highway, Charleston

1 qt. apple juice
1 qt. apple cider
1 C. salt
1/2 C. garlic powder
1/2 C. onion powder
1 C. Worcestershire sauce

1 C. vegetable oil
1 Tbsp ground thyme
1 tsp black pepper
1/2 tsp cayenne pepper (optional)
1 C. prepared mustard

1. Combine all ingredients, and mix well.

2. Baste the pork four to six hours before cooking, almost as a marinade, and every 30 minutes while cooking. Be sure to use a sanitized brush each time you baste to avoid cross contamination.

{ *Dr. Alexander Garden, a Charleston physician first imported "Cape Jasmine" from South Africa in about 1754. The flower was renamed Gardenia after Dr. Garden.* }

Fried Green Tomatoes
Blind Tiger Pub
38/36 Broad St, Charleston

4 large green tomatoes, sliced ¼" thick
1 ½ C. AP flour
½ C. buttermilk
2 eggs, beaten
1 C. panko bread crumbs
salt and pepper to taste
Canola oil for frying

Basil Aoili:
3/4 C. mayonnaise
1/3 C. finely chopped fresh basil
1 Tbsp fresh lemon juice
1 1/2 tsp minced garlic
1 1/2 tsp grated lemon peel

1. Combine flour, salt and pepper in a large bowl and set aside

2. Combine buttermilk and eggs.

3. Dredge the tomato slices first in the flour, then in the egg mixture, and finally in the panko crumbs (dry-wet-dry).

4. Fry slices in canola oil at 350°F, for 3-5 minutes, turning once to brown evenly.

Aoili:

1. Mix all ingredients in medium bowl. Season to taste with salt and pepper.

2. Cover and refrigerate at least 1 hour to allow flavors to develop. (Can be prepared 2 days ahead. Keep refrigerated.)

Frogmore Stew
Bowen's Island Restaurant
1870 Bowens Island Rd., Charleston

2 lbs fresh shrimp, peeled & deveined
1 ½ – 2 lbs Hillshire Farms sausage
1 ½ lbs small red potatoes

6 ears corn, broken in half
3 Tbsp Old Bay seasoning
dash of Texas Pete (optional)

1. Fill large pot ¼ full of water. Add Old Bay and Texas Pete.

2. When water starts to boil, add potatoes and cook about 10 minutes or until potatoes are easy to pierce with fork.

3. Add sausage and cook for about 5 minutes.

4. With the water still boiling, add the shrimp. Cut off heat and stir until the shrimp are a little pink. Drain.

The key to good Frogmore stew is to make certain not to overcook the shrimp. Because there is a lot of heat in the potatoes, corn, and sausage, the shrimp will continue to cook after you drain the stew.

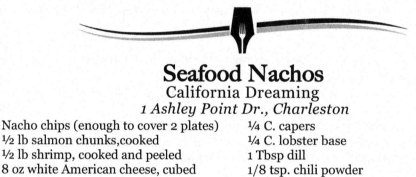

Seafood Nachos
California Dreaming
1 Ashley Point Dr., Charleston

Nacho chips (enough to cover 2 plates)
½ lb salmon chunks, cooked
½ lb shrimp, cooked and peeled
8 oz white American cheese, cubed
8 oz heavy cream
½ C. diced red onion

¼ C. capers
¼ C. lobster base
1 Tbsp dill
1/8 tsp. chili powder
1/8 tsp. paprika

1. Heat the heavy cream, lobster base and cheese in a large sauce pan over medium heat, stirring constantly until mixture is completely melted.

2. Add onions and capers and simmer for 10 minutes until onions are soft.

3. Add salmon and shrimp, stirring gently.

4. Add dill and chili powder, stir in and remove from heat.

5. Put a layer of chips on an ovenproof plate, then a generous helping of seafood mixture. Continue with a second layer.

6. Place under a broiler to brown.

7. Garnish with paprika and serve hot!

King Charles II of England gave the Carolina territory to eight loyal friends then collectively known as the "Lords Proprietor" in 1663. Their first Carolina settlement was "Charles Town" named after King Charles which would later be shortened to "Charleston". The community was established in 1670 across the Ashley River from Charleston's present-day location.

World Famous "Crab House" Crab Pot
Charleston Crab House
Charleston, South Carolina

Scampi Butter:
3 large cloves garlic, peeled
1 green onion, chopped
2 Tbsp fresh parsley leaves
1 Tbsp lemon juice
½ cup unsalted butter, melted
salt & pepper to taste

Crab Pot:
2 lbs snow crab legs, thawed
2 lbs Dungeness crab legs, thawed
2 lbs shrimp, 21/25 count, peeled & deveined

40 mussels
4 pieces fresh corn on the cob, shucked & cut in half
10 red skin potatoes, cut in half
2 yellow sweet onions. peeled & cut in half
1 lb smoked sausage, cut in 2" pieces
scampi butter
cocktail sauce
lemon wedges
cocktail fork
crab cracker

Scampi Butter:

1. In a mixing bowl, combine garlic, onion and parsley. Mix in lemon juice and butter until thoroughly combined. Season with salt & pepper. Use immediately or store in the refrigerator until ready to use.

Crab Pot:

1. In a large pot, steam potatoes, corn, sausage and onion for 10 minutes.

2. Add crab legs and cook for 3 minutes.

3. Add mussels and cook for 2 minutes. Everything should be submerged in boiling water – if not, add more hot water to cover.

4. Add shrimp and continue steaming for another 3-5 minutes.

5. Strain and place in serving dish. Pour scampi butter on top. Garnish with cocktail fork, lemon wedge and cocktail sauce. Oh and don't forget your Crab cracker!

The Angel Oak Tree is a Southern live oak located in Angel Oak Park on Johns Island near Charleston, South Carolina. The Angel Oak Tree is estimated to be at least 400 and as much as 1400-1500 years old.

Shrimp and Grits
Charleston Grill
224 King St., Charleston

Shrimp
8 shrimp, peeled and de-veined
1 tsp. garlic, chopped
2 tsp. shallots, chopped
1 yellow tomato, peeled, seeded and diced
1 tbsp. olive oil
1 tbsp. Opal basil, chopped fine
1/2-cup dry white wine
1/4 cup heavy cream
Salt and fresh ground white pepper, to taste

Grits
2 1/2 tbsp. unsalted butter
2 1/4 cups chicken stock
1/2 cup Charleston Grill stone ground grits
1 to 2 cups heavy cream
Salt and fresh cracked white pepper, to taste
1 Tsp. fresh lemon zest, chopped fine

Shrimp:

1. Salt and pepper the shrimp on each side. In a large pan, heat the olive oil and then add the shrimp.

2. Cook for one minute on each side and remove from the pan.

3. Add the garlic and shallots and cook for another 30 seconds.

4. Add the tomatoes and the white wine. Reduce the wine by half and add the cream. Reduce to a sauce consistency.

5.Return the shrimp to the sauce and add the Opal basil. Salt and pepper to taste and pour this over the hot grits.

Grits:

1. Bring the chicken stock and butter to a boil in a thick-bottomed saucepan.

2. Stir in the grits and return to a boil.

3. Reduce the heat, allowing the grits to cook for another 15 minutes at a low boil, and until the grits are thick and have absorbed most of the chicken stock. Stir occasionally to keep the grits from sticking.

4. Add 1/2 cup of the heavy cream to the pot and reduce the heat, allowing the grits to cook slowly for another 10 minutes.

5. As the liquid is absorbed, add more cream, cooking the grits until thick and full-bodied.

6. Add salt and pepper to taste with a total cooking time of at least an hour.

Located in the Battery of downtown Charleston is White Point Gardens, which received its name from the English in 1670. As they sailed along the coast of Charleston, they noticed droves of white oyster shells in this area, which is why the called it "White Point."

Truffle Spoon Bread
Circa 1886
149 Wentworth St., Charleston

Tomato Jelly:
10 Roma tomatoes, peeled
¾ C. sugar
1 large red bell pepper, roasted, seeded & peeled
¼ C. fresh orange juice
6 Tbsp lemon juice
3 cloves garlic, peeled
1 shallot
¼ tsp Tabasco
¼ tsp dried basil
pinch crushed red pepper flakes

Parmesan Tuiles:
1 lb parmesan cheese, grated
1 large summer truffle, minced fine

Spoon Bread:
4 C. milk
1 Tbsp white truffle oil
1 C. cornmeal
2 Tbsp butter
1 ¾ tsp salt
white pepper to taste
4 eggs, separated
2 ½ cups cooked spaghetti squash, loosely packed
3 Tbsp summer truffle, minced
fresh chives, minced
micro mustard greens (available at The Chef's Garden)
clarified butter

Tomato Jelly:

1. Place all ingredients into a saucepot, cooking over a moderate heat, stirring occasionally. Cook until everything is very soft and then pulse with a hand blender so that the mixture resembles jam. Cool and reserve for use.

Parmesan Tuiles:

1. Place the shredded parmesan in the shapes of triangles onto a silpat. Garnish with the minced truffles and bake in a convection oven at 350°F for 3-7 minutes. Keep a close eye on them; pull and cool completely.

Spoon Bread:

1. Cut spaghetti squash in half. Season with salt & white pepper and brush with clarified butter. Bake on a sheet tray, flesh side down, at 325°F convection oven for 20-35 minutes or until fork tender. Once cooked, "pull" and scrape out the flesh with a fork and set aside.

2. Lightly beat the egg yolks, set aside. Scald the milk and stir in the cornmeal. Cook this mixture for 3 minutes stirring constantly. Add the butter, truffle oil, salt and beaten egg yolks. Fold the spaghetti squash into the cornmeal mixture. Next whip the whites until light and fluffy and fold this into the cornmeal base. Add minced chives and truffles.

3. Place a ring mold atop a small cast iron pan and spoon mixture into it. Bake in a 350°F convection oven for 12-15 minutes. It should look like a firm soufflé when done.

4. Once cooked, run a knife around the ring mold and pull it off the spoon bread. Serve immediately garnished with the tomato jam spooned on top, then micro mustard greens and finally the parmesan tuile.

Bacon Popcorn & Old-Fashioned Cocktail
Cocktail Club
479 King St #200, Charleston

Bacon Popcorn:
1 Tbsp bacon fat
¼ tsp paprika
1/8 tsp cayenne pepper
½ tsp brown sugar
1 tsp salt
1 Tbsp olive oil
Popcorn for popping

Old-Fashioned Cocktail:
2 brandied cherries
½ orange slice
¾ oz. simple syrup
3 oz. rye whiskey
Angostura or Peychaud bitters
soda water
lemon peel

Bacon Popcorn:

1. Combine all ingredients except the popcorn in a sauce pan over low heat.

2. Prepare a batch of popcorn, preferably in large boiler using peanut oil.

3. Pour the sauce mix over the popcorn and toss. Serve hot!

Old-Fashioned Cocktail:

1. Muddle cherries, orange and simple syrup in a tall glass, then fill with ice.

2. Add rye whiskey and stir with a spoon.

3. Add several dashes of bitters, to taste, and stir.

4. Pour into a double old-fashioned glass, and top with a splash of soda water.

5. Squeeze and twist the lemon over the cocktail, and rum along the rim of the glass.

{ *The first fried fish was introduced to Charleston in early 1700's, not from England, but from Jewish refugees from Portugal and Spain.* }

Smokehouse Fried Catfish
Cumberland Street Smokehouse
5 Cumberland St. Charleston

6 Catfish filets
Marinade:
½ C. Texas Pete
½ C. Squire's yellow mustard
½ C. whole grain creole mustard

Dredge:
3 C. Wondra flour
2/3 C. Stone Ground Corn meal
3 Tbsp Old Bay seasoning
Oil for frying

1. Mix marinade together and add filets making sure each piece of fish is well coated.

2. Marinate for at least 1 hour.

3. Mix together dredge and one at a time press the filets firmly into the dredge until evenly coated.

4. Deep fry at 375 degrees F for about 4 min or until golden brown.

5. Serve with you favorite tarter sauce and hushpuppies.

Hoppin' John
Dave's Carry-Out
42 Morris St, Charleston

2 strips thick-cut bacon, cut into ½"
pieces
2 cloves garlic, finely chopped
1 rib celery, finely chopped
½ large yellow onion, finely chopped
½ large green bell pepper, stemmed,
seeded, and finely chopped
Kosher salt and freshly ground black
pepper, to taste
1 cup long-grain white rice, rinsed

1 tsp. dried thyme
1 tsp. ground cumin
1 tsp. ground coriander
2 whole cloves
1 stick cinnamon
1 bay leaf
2½ cups chicken stock
1 15-oz. can black-eyed peas, rinsed
Freshly grated nutmeg, to taste

1. Heat oven to 350°.

2. Heat bacon in a 6-qt. saucepan over medium-high heat; cook, stirring, until fat renders, about 4 minutes.

3. Add garlic, celery, onion, and pepper, salt, and pepper, and cook, stirring, until soft, about 4 minutes.

4. Add rice, thyme, cumin, coriander, cloves, cinnamon, and bay leaf, and cook until rice is lightly toasted, about 3 minutes.

5. Add stock and bring to a boil. Cover pan with lid and place in oven; bake until liquid is absorbed and rice is cooked through, about 20 minutes.

6. Stir in black-eyed peas and nutmeg and let sit, covered, for 10 minutes.

The Arthur Ravenel, Jr. bridge was constructed to replace the deteriorating John P. Grace Memorial Bridge and Silas N. Pearman Bridge in spanning the Cooper River. This is the longest cable-stayed bridge in North America.

Shrimp & Crab Hoppin' John
Fat Hen
3140 Maybank Hwy, Johns Island

Beans:
2 C. dried black eyed peas
1 ham hock
4 C. water
Rice:
1 C. long-grain rice
1 medium yellow onion, diced
7 strips apple wood smoked bacon, diced
2 Tbsp sweet butter
½ C. green onion, minced
2 Tbsp lemon juice
hot sauce

salt & pepper to taste

Shrimp & Crab:
1 tsp olive oil
2 oz. white wine
3 oz. chicken stock
¼ oz. zucchini, julienned
¼ oz. squash, julienned
¼ oz. carrot, julienned
1 oz. garlic butter
50 shrimp, peeled & deveined
2 oz. jumbo lump crab meat

Beans:

1. Rinse beans and place in a medium sauce pot and cover with water.

2. Add ham hock and bring to a boil and cook until tender (to speed up cooking time, soak beans overnight). When beans are tender, strain and cool. Reserve ham hock.

3. When cooled, pick meat off of ham hock and add back to the beans.

Rice:

1. Render the bacon and sweat the onion until tender. Add butter and melt.

2. Add rice and cook for 30 seconds. Cover rice with water (about 1 inch). Cook until all liquid is gone and rice is tender. Spread the rice mixture on a sheet tray and cool.

3. Mix rice, beans and green onion together. Season with hot sauce, salt, pepper and lemon juice. Remember, the mixture is cold, so do not over season. When the dish is heated back up, the flavors will awaken.

Shrimp & Crab:

1. In a sauté pan, add olive oil and heat to smoking point. Add shrimp, sauté on both sides just to color, then remove from pan.

2. Deglaze pan with white wine. Add vegetables, hoppin' john and chicken stock.

3. Add shrimp back to the pan along with the crab meat.

4. Finish with garlic butter and season with salt & pepper.

5. Check seasoning. Place on your favorite serving platter and garnish with chopped parsley.

If you look closely at some of the buildings in downtown Charleston you will notice metal circles or disks (about the size of a plate) on the exterior. These circles are actually the ends of earthquake rods. These rods or bolts were added to newly constructed buildings after the devastating Charleston earthquake of 1886, in hopes to strengthening building structures.

BBQ Collards
Fiery Ron's Home Team BBQ
Sullivan's Island and West Ashley

1 gallon water
3 C. cider vinegar
¼ C. hot sauce
½ C. brown sugar
½ C. kosher salt

2 to 3 shoulder bones or smoked ham hocks
½ lb smoked pork shoulder, chopped or pulled
2 lbs collard greens, cut in 2" strips

1. Bring water to a simmer.
2. Add cider vinegar, hot sauce, brown sugar and kosher salt.
3. Add bones or ham hocks for flavor and simmer for 25 minutes.
4. Add greens and smoked pork.
5. Simmer lightly for 2-3 hours or until tender.

The modern monolithic Sullivan's Island Lighthouse, the last major lighthouse built by the federal government in 1962, resembles an air traffic control tower more than a traditional lighthouse. The tower's unique triangular shape, with one point directed towards the ocean, allows it to withstand winds of up to 125 miles per hour.

Coddled Sea Island Farm Egg With Stone Crab

FIG

232 Meeting St, Charleston

8 6-8 oz ramekins or small cocottes
8 locally sourced eggs
1 lb picked fresh stone crab meat (you can substitute lump crab)
1 C. English peas, blanched
(I substituted Lady peas that were cooked for about 10 minutes)
4 thin slices of country ham or prosciutto, julienned (I used prosciutto)
1 C. parmesan-truffle cream (recipe follows)
1 qt parsnip cream (recipe follows)
3 Tbsp butter
1 Tbsp fresh snipped chives
sea salt

I loaf of brioche, sliced and lightly toasted

Parmesan-Truffle cream:
1 C. heavy cream
2 oz piece parmesan rind
2 drops of black truffle oil
pinch salt

Parsnip cream:
2 C. parsnips, peeled, diced
1 small leek, white part only, diced
1 C. whole milk
3/4 C. heavy cream
fresh bay leaf
1 tsp salt

For Parmesan-Truffle Cream:

1. Combine all ingredients and simmer lightly for five minutes and let stand till cool.

2. Strain, reserve.

For Parsnip cream:

1. Combine all ingredients and simmer very lightly until all ingredients are tender.

2. Remove bay leaf and puree in blender until silky smooth. Place the parsnip mixture into a small pan and cover with plastic wrap. Keep warm.

Assembly:

1. Preheat oven to 325. Place the ramekins in a deep casserole and fill it up with hot water halfway up the sides. Put 2 ounces of parsnip cream into each ramekin.

2. Crack a farm egg into a coffee cup or ramekin one at a time and slide it onto the parsnip cream.

3. When all the eggs are in, place the casserole into the oven. The eggs should take about 8-10 minutes, they are finished when the white is firm and the yolk is runny. It is important not to leave the kitchen during this time. The eggs can go from perfect to overdone in a matter of seconds.

4. In the meantime, melt the butter in a nice sauté pan. Swirl it around over medium hat until it begins to foam up and brown.

5. Add the picked stone crab, the peas and country ham. Warm through and season with salt and finish with the snipped chives.

6. When the eggs are done, divide the stone crab over the top of each mixture, top with the Parmesan-Truffle cream and sprinkle with a touch of sea salt. Serve with toasted brioche.

{
A sea captain would spear a pineapple to his fence post to let friends know he was home safely and to please visit so he could regale his guests with tales of the high seas. The pineapple today is a symbol of hospitality.
}

Sweet Tea Vodka Lemonade Mojitos
Firefly Distillery
6775 Bears Bluff Rd, Wadmalaw Island

1 lemon (Use a meyer lemon, if you can find one!)
10-12 fresh mint leaves
ice

4 oz. Firefly Sweet Tea vodka
1 cup lemonade

1. Squeeze each half of the lemon into two 16oz mason jars or tumblers then place lemon half in glass.

2. Add 5-6 fresh mint leaves to each glass then muddle with a wooden spoon.

3. Fill glasses with ice then add 2oz sweet tea vodka and 1/2 cup lemonade to each glass.

4. Screw on top and shake to combine or stir to combine then serve.

To make ahead: Muddle lemon and mint in mason jars then add vodka and lemonade. Screw on top then refrigerate until ready to drink. Add ice then shake and serve.

The Palmetto is rooted in historical significance dating back to the Revolutionary War. On June 28, 1776, the British fleet's attack on Sullivan's Island was repulsed. The palmetto-log fort, under Colonel William Moultrie, withstood the barrage of British cannons until the fleet retreated.

Stuffed Hush Puppies
Fleet Landing
186 Concord St, Charleston

3 cups heavy cream
2 1/2 C. water
2 C. lobster stock
1 C. crab stock
salt and freshly ground black pepper
4 sticks plus 2 tbs unsalted butter
3 ears fresh corn shucked and kernels cut off
3 leeks (white parts only) washed and finely julienned
3 1/2 C. all-purpose flour
1 1/2 tsp Old Bay Seasoning

Pinch of cayenne pepper
pinch of freshly ground white pepper
1/4 tsp ground cumin
1-1 lb box of hush puppy mix (you may need other ingredients-check the package)
4 C. peanut oil
12 large (26-30 count) shrimp, peeled and deveined
2 C. fresh lobster meat
1/2 C. white wine
fresh parsley, chopped (optional)

1. Begin by preparing the veloute sauce. In a large pot, bring the cream, water, lobster and crab stock, and salt and pepper to a low boil over high heat. In the meantime, melt 1 pound of butter in a large soup pot or stockpot over medium-high heat . Add the corn kernels and leeks to the melted butter pot, stirring, and cook over medium heat until both begetables are just softened, about 5 minutes. Add the flour all at once, stirring to coat the vegetables evenly. Cook for about 3 minutes, and then gradually incorporate the simmering liquid mixture, stirring well to avoid lumps. Add the Old Bay Seasoning, cayenne pepper, white pepper, and cumin. Stir to incorporate, then reduce the heat to low and simmer the veloute until it is thick enough to coat the back of a spoon, about 12 minutes.

2. Meanwhile, prepare the hush puppy batter according to the manufacturer's directions. Heat the peanut oil to 350 degrees in a fryer or a deep skillet. Once the oil is hot, scoop the batter, using a large ice-cream scoop, into the oil Fry until the hush puppies are about one quarter of the way done, about 2 minutes. Remove from the fryer and drain on paper towels. When they are cool enough to handle, cut a small piece off the bottom of each puppy with a serrated knife. This will create a steady base for the puppy to sit on. Next, cut a 1/4 inch thick slice off the top of each, and with a small fork, gently remove the raw batter in the center, leaving a sturdy 1/4 inch thick wall. Set the puppies and their tops aside.

3. To finish the veloute, melt the remaining 2 tbs of butter over the medium heat in a large pot. Add the shrimp and lobster. Saute, tossing, until the seafood is almost translucent, about 4 minutes. Deglaze the pot with the white wine and reduce until the wine forms a glaze, about 1 minute. Add the simmering vegetable veloute sauce and stir. Taste and adjust salt and pepper as needed.

4. Return the cored hush puppies (but not the tops) to the hot oil and fry until completely cooked and golden, another 5 or 6 minutes. Remove with a slotted spoon and briefly drain on paper towels. Using a small soup spoon, fill each puppy with veloute and replace the reserved tops. Serve immediately, placing 2 hush puppies on each shallow plate. Garnish, if desired, with a sprinkle of fresh chopped parsley. Enjoy!!

Double Chocolate Pound Cake
The Glass Onion
1219 Savannah Hwy, Charleston

2 ½ C. sugar
8 farm eggs
1 Tbsp vanilla
2 tsp salt
1 lb unsalted butter, melted
2 ¼ C. cake flour
¾ C. cocoa

2 tsp baking powder
1 ½ C. chocolate chips tossed in cocoa powder
Glaze:
1 C. sugar
¾ C. water
1 tsp vanilla

1. Preheat oven to 350 degrees.

2. Grease and dust a Bundt pan with cocoa powder.

3. Combine sugar, eggs, vanilla and salt in a food processor. Mix until combined.

4. While running pour butter into mixture and continue running until thoroughly combined.

5. Pour this mixture into a large mixing bowl.

6. Sift dry ingredients into wet ingredients, whisking as you go.

7. Add chocolate chips and stir to combine.

8. Pour batter into pan. Bake until a tester comes out clean, about 1 hour.

9. Remove from oven and allow to cool for 10 minutes.

10. Release from pan and brush with glaze. Once cool cut into 16 slices.

Glaze:

1. Combine ingredients and cook over low heat until sugar dissolves and syrup forms.

2. Brush onto cake.

Fried Green Tomatoes with Crab & Shrimp
Halls Chophouse
434 King St., Charleston

1 lb apple wood smoked bacon, sliced
2 C. roasted corn, cut off cob
2 C. fresh tomatoes, diced
olive oil
1 Tbsp blackening seasoning
1 C. heavy cream
½ lb lump crab meat & small shrimp

6 green tomatoes, sliced ¼" thick
1 C. buttermilk
1 C. cornmeal
2 C. all-purpose flour
2 Tbsp Old Bay
salt & pepper to taste

1. In large saucepan, cook bacon, corn and tomatoes in a little olive oil over medium heat for 10 minutes.

2. Add blackening seasoning and heavy cream; simmer on low until reduced by half.

3. Stir in shrimp and crabmeat and add salt & pepper to taste.

4. Soak tomato slices in buttermilk.

5. Combine cornmeal, flour and Old Bay in bowl.

6. Dredge tomato slices in breading mixture and fry in olive oil until golden brown.

7. Top with shrimp and crab mixture.

Curried Shrimp
Hank's Seafood
10 Hayne St. Charleston

2 C. carrots
2 C. celery
2 C. onion
2 C. leeks
3 cans chicken broth
1 Tbsp garlic, minced

1/2 C. curry Madras powder
2 ripe bananas, pureed
2 C. cream
1 lb shrimp
4 qt rice, cooked

1. Dice carrots, celery, onions and leeks and sauté.

2. Add chicken broth, garlic, curry powder, bananas and cream.

3. Add shrimp until cooked.

4. Add sauce to rice and serve.

Blue Crab Butterbean Soup
High Cotton
199 E Bay St., Charleston

For soup:
2 C. yellow squash, medium chop
1 large red bell pepper, small chop
1 large white onion, small chop
1 1/2 C. cooked butterbeans or lima beans, blanched
1/2 lb smoked sausage, medium chop
1 fresh jalapeno, minced

1 Tbsp garlic, minced
1 Tbsp creole seasoning
to taste tabasco
to taste salt
4 C. chicken stock
3 Tbsp butter
1 lb picked blue crab

1. In a medium pot, melt Butter.

2. Add squash, red pepper, onion and jalapeno.

3. Sauté for 5 minutes.

4. Add sausage, beans, garlic and Creole seasoning.

5. Simmer 5 minutes.

6. Add stock and salt, season to taste.

7. Simmer 30 minutes.

For topping:

1. Sauté the 1 pound of blue crab in butter with a pinch of parsley, lemon, and salt and pepper to taste.

2. Divide evenly amongst the bowls and garnish with a pinch of cornbread crumbles and cup chopped scallions.

Shrimp Burgers
Hominy Grill
207 Rutledge Ave., Charleston

1 rib celery
4 to 6 stems flat-leaf parsley
2 to 3 scallions (root ends trimmed)
1 large lemon
1 lb cooked, peeled and deveined shrimp
(thoroughly defrosted, if using frozen)
3 Tbsp low-fat mayonnaise

1 cup packed cornbread crumbs
kosher salt
freshly ground black pepper
hot pepper sauce, such as Tabasco
1 large egg
1 Tbsp peanut oil

1. Line a large plate with a few layers of paper towels.

2. Cut the celery into 1/4-inch (or smaller) dice to yield 3 tablespoons and place in a large mixing bowl. Add the following ingredients to the bowl as you work: Finely chop the parsley to yield 2 tablespoons. Cut the white and light-green scallion parts crosswise into thin slices to yield at least 2 tablespoons. Finely grate the zest of the lemon to yield 1 1/2 teaspoons; reserve the lemon for another use. Finely chop the shrimp (discarding the tails); this can be done by hand, or half of the shrimp can be processed briefly in a food processor to vary the texture of the burgers.

3. Add the mayonnaise and cornbread crumbs, stirring to combine. Season with salt, pepper and hot pepper sauce to taste; mix well. Add the egg and stir until well incorporated; the mixture should barely hold together as you form eight 4-inch burgers.

4. Heat the oil in a large skillet, preferably nonstick, over medium-high heat until the oil shimmers. Add 4 of the burgers and cook for 3 to 4 minutes, until lightly browned on the bottom, then use 2 spatulas to carefully turn them over and cook for 3 to 4 minutes, until evenly browned. Transfer to the paper towel-lined plate; cover loosely with aluminum foil to keep them warm. Repeat with the remaining 4 burgers.

Serve on soft, warm hamburger buns or on top of lightly dressed salad greens.

On December 20, 1860, the South Carolina legislature was the first southern state to vote for secession from the Federal Union primarily because Abraham Lincoln's purposes were deemed "hostile to continued slavery".

On January 9, 1861, Cadets from the Citadel, South Carolina's liberal arts military college fired the first shots of the Civil War on a Union ship entering Charleston Harbor. On April 12, 1961, South Carolina Confederate forces fired on the Union held Fort Sumter in the harbor. After 34-hours of continuous bombardment, Union forces surrendered Fort Sumter.

Green Gobble'n

HOM
563 King St, Charleston, SC

Turkey patty
Melted leeks & spinach
Brie cheese

Green goddess aioli
Green apples

1. Sear 6.5oz turkey patty on both sides in pre-heated pan with 1 tablespoon of vegetable oil.

2. Transfer to sheet pan and put in 375-degree oven.

3. Cook until internal temperature of 165 degrees.

4. Toast brioche bun and assemble as follows. Bun, melted leeks & spinach, turkey patty, brie cheese, aioli, green apples.

Green Goddess Aioli

HOM
563 King St, Charleston, SC

3/4 C. egg yolk
1 Tbsp garlic cloves, crushed
1 Tbsp Dijon mustard
.1/3 C. lemon juice
1 3/4 Tbsp salt
1/2 C. water

1 bunch cilantro, rough chop
1/2 bunch parsley, rough chop
1 bunch mint, rough chop
1 bunch basil, rough chop
1/2 C. chives, minced
5 C. vegetable oil

1. Add all ingredients, EXCEPT for oil, into a blender and begin to puree.

2. Slowly drizzle oil into running blender until it thickens.

3. Check seasoning for salt and may need a little cold water to thin out.

Spinach & Leeks

HOM
563 King St, Charleston, SC

4 leeks, halved & sliced
.1/2 stick butter
1 Tbsp garlic, minced

2 1/2 lb. spinach
1/2 C. white wine
salt & pepper to taste

1. Cut leeks at the white/green part and discard green leek tops. Discard the root as well.

2. Split whites lengthwise and slice into thin half circles.

3. Place into a container with enough water to float the leeks, agitate and allow to dirt to settle.

4. Strain and rinse again in strainer.

5. In large stockpot, allow butter to melt over moderate heat, add strained leeks and allow to sweat while stirring for several minutes until softened.

6. Add minced garlic and allow to cook out a couple minutes.

7. Fill stockpot with spinach and add white wine, cover and melt spinach. Stirring occasionally.

8. Once cooked down, season and then strain. Discard cooking liquid.

Turkey Burger
HOM
161 East Bay Street, Charleston

6 lb. ground turkey
1 yellow onion, small dice
1 stalk celery, small dice
1 tsp garlic, minced
5 sprigs thyme, chopped

5 sprigs rosemary, chopped
¼ bunch parsley, chopped
salt & pepper to taste
½ cup bread crumbs

1. Sweat onion & celery until soft and translucent.

2. Add garlic and sauté briefly.

3. Allow this to cool.

4. Mix all ingredients together and season with S&P. It may require more bread crumbs for firmer consistency.

5. Portion to 6.5oz and refrigerate.

The inventor of Charleston's She Crab Soup was William Deas, a butler and a cook to R. Goodwyn Rhett, mayor of Charleston. According the local legend, William Howard Taft, 27th president of the United States, was being "wined and dined" by Mayor R. Rhett at the home of one of the original signers of the United States Constitution, John Rutledge. Supposedly, the Rhetts' asked their butler to "dress up" the pale crab soup they usually served. The butler added orange-hued crab eggs to give color and improve the flavor, thus inventing the Charleston delicacy know as She Crab Soup.

She-Crab Soup
Hyman's Seafood
Charleston, South Carolina

2 ½ C. milk
1 lb crabmeat
½ C. celery, finely diced
1 Tbsp chicken base
½ C. heavy cream

4 tsp sherry
½ onion, diced
2 ½ C. flour
1 stick butter

1. Sauté onions and celery with butter in a saucepan.

2. Add flour and stir until thick.

3. Add heavy cream and chicken base. Bring to a boil stirring occasionally.

4. Add crabmeat and simmer for 5 minutes.

5. Add milk to get desired the consistency.

6. Top each serving with teaspoon of sherry.

Maple Leaf Duck Breast
Indigo Grille
20 Patriots Point Rd., Mount Pleasant

For Espresso Chile Duck Rub:
1 dbl pod Espresso Grounds (14g)
¼ C. Chile Powder
¼ C. Paprika
2 Tbsp brown sugar
1 Tbsp ground mustard
2 Tbsp smoked kosher salt
1 Tbsp black pepper
2 Tbsp coriander
1 Tbsp ginger
2 tsp cayenne

For Pickled Beet Slaw Brine:
1 C. rice wine vinegar
4 Tbsp sugar
4 Tbsp olive oil
½ tsp dry mustard
salt & pepper, to taste

For Pickled Beet Slaw:
2 beets
2 carrots
1 yellow pepper
¼ head red cabbage
(all julienne cut)

For Chimichurri:
2 bunches cilantro
1 bunch parsley
5 ea garlic cloves
5 ea Jalapenos, seeded
1 Tbsp coriander
2 ea limes, juiced
½ C. red wine vinegar
2 Tbsp honey
6 ea peppercorns
1 Tbsp salt

Espresso Chile Duck Rub:

1. Mix thoroughly - do not toast.

Pickled Beet Slaw:

1. Bring all brine ingredients to boil and dissolve sugar.

2. While HOT pour over slaw ingredients.

Chimichurri:

1. Blend until smooth.

Maple Leaf Duck Breast:

1. Lightly score duck and coat with espresso rub.

2. Pan sear in cast iron skillet skin side fi rst for 3 minutes on each side.

3. Let duck rest for 5 minutes before slicing.

4. Place a small amount of mesclun greens in a bowl and toss with pickled beet slaw.

Charleston boasts several firsts...
the first public college, The College of Charleston,
founded in 1770;
the first museum, The Charleston Museum,
founded in 1773
and the first playhouse, the Dock Street Theatre,
founded in 1736.
All are still operating today.

Coca Cola Cake
Jestine's Kitchen
251 Meeting St., Charleston

Ingredients for cake:
2 C. self-rising flour
2 C. sugar
3 Tbsp cocoa
1 C. Coca-Cola
1 C. butter
1 1/2 C. miniature marshmallows
2 eggs, beaten
1/2 C. buttermilk

1 tsp baking soda
1 tsp vanilla extract

Frosting:
1/2 C. butter
1 Tbsp cocoa
6 Tbsp Coca-Cola
1 lb box confectioner's sugar

1. Grease and flour a 9 x 13-inch pan and set aside. In a large bowl combine flour and sugar. In a saucepan combine the cocoa, Coca-Cola, butter, and marshmallows; bring to a boil. Combine the boiled mixture with the flour and sugar mixture.

2. In a separate bowl mix eggs, buttermilk, baking soda, and vanilla; add to the first mixture. Pour into prepared pan and bake at 350 degrees for about 35 minutes, until cake tests done.

3. For frosting: in a saucepan, bring butter, cocoa, and Coca-Cola to a boil. Stir in the sugar and mix well. Spread over the cake while both cake and frosting are still warm. Makes about 16 servings.

She-Crab Soup
John Rutledge House Inn
116 Broad St., Charleston

5 Tbsp butter
1/2 C. finely chopped celery
2 C. crab meat
3 1/2 C. milk
1/2 C. chicken stock
5 Tbsp. flour
2/3 tsp mace
1/4 tsp white pepper

1 C. heavy cream
1/4 C. Worcestershire
3 Tbsp dry sherry
salt if necessary, to taste

Optional: 2 hard boiled egg yolks, grated
+ paprika

1. Heat butter in large sauce pan. Add celery, mace and white pepper.

2. Cook over low heat until celery is almost transparent. While celery is cooking, heat milk and chicken stock in small pan just enough to make milk hot without boiling. When celery mix is done, add flour to make a roux. Do not brown but heat enough to bubble for several minutes.

3. Slowly add milk and chicken stock to roux, add salt for taste. Add crab mean, heavy cream, Worcestershire, and sherry. Simmer for 30 minutes or until thickened to appropriate consistency.

4. For a garnish boil 2 eggs. Take the yolk out and grate. Sprinkle over the tops with paprika.

Hummingbird Cake
Kaminsky's
78 N Market St., Charleston

3 C. flour
1 C. oil
2 C. sugar
1 tsp. soda
2 C. chopped nuts
3 eggs
1 tsp. salt
1 ½ tsp. vanilla
1 tsp. cinnamon

1 8-oz.can crushed pineapple with juice
2 C. chopped - not mashed - bananas

Icing:
1 8-oz. pkg. cream cheese
1 stick butter
1 tsp. vanilla
1 box powdered sugar
1 C. chopped nuts

1. Preheat oven to 350. Grease and flour a bundt pan or 2 9-inch round pans.
2. Mix dry ingredients together. Beat eggs with oil and add, along with vanilla, and pineapple. Do not beat. Fold in banana chunks. Bake for 1 hour 10 minutes; cool in pan and remove.

Icing:
1. Beat together til smooth, fold in nuts.
Note: For layer cake, double the icing recipe.

Shrimp Fritter
Library at Vendue Inn
19 Vendue Range, Charleston

3 1/4 C. all-purpose flour
2 tsp baking powder
1 tsp kosher salt
1/2 tsp cayenne pepper
3 whole eggs, beaten
1 1/2 C. milk

1 Tbsp olive oil
1/2 C. yellow onion, small dice
1 Tbsp garlic, minced
1 lb cooked shrimp
1 Tbsp flat leaf parsley

1. In a large bowl, combine the dry ingredients.
2. In a separate bowl, combine the wet ingredients. Set both aside.
3. Heat oil in a medium sauté pan and sauté vegetables until the onion is just cooked. Don't brown
the garlic.
4. Whisk wet ingredients into dry ingredients.
5. Add the vegetables, shrimp and parsley. Combine thoroughly.
6. Spoon a small amount into a heated, lightly oiled non-stick skillet.
7. When bubbles begin to form in batter on the top side, flip to brown on the other side.
8. Cook for about 1 more minute and remove from heat.

Charleston Crabcakes
Magnolia's
185 East Bay St., Charleston

1/2 C. minced red onions
1/3 C. minced red bell pepper
1 Tbsp minced tarragon
1/3 C. mayonnaise
1 lb jumbo lump or lump crabmeat, gently picked over and drained of any liquid

3/4 C. panko
2 tsp salt or to taste
1/4 tsp white pepper
1/8 tsp cayenne pepper
6 Tbsp light olive oil

1. Place onions, bell pepper, tarragon and mayonnaise in a mixing bowl and combine. Gently fold in the crabmeat. Add the panko and season with salt, white pepper and cayenne pepper to taste. Let the mixture rest for 5 minutes. The panko will absorb some of the moisture and the mixture will stay together.

2. Lay out a large piece of plastic wrap on a clean counter surface. Place half of the crab mixture on it and use a spatula or a spoon to form it into a tube about 1 3/4 inches in diameter. Bring the wrap up over the crab and roll the crab mixture up. Twist the ends to close. Pierce any air pockets with a toothpick or skewer. Twist the ends even tighter to compress the crab mixture. Tuck under the ends of the wrap and place the tube on a plate. Repeat with the second half of the crab cake mixture. Place the tubes in the refrigerator for at least 1 hour or overnight.

When Ready To Cook:

1. Preheat oven to 350 degrees.

2. When ready to use, cut the tubes into 1 1/4-inch-thick cakes. Gently remove the plastic wrap, leaving the cakes in nice cylinders.

3. Heat 3 tablespoons oil in a heavy-bottomed frying pan (non-stick works well here) over medium-high heat until very hot, but not smoking. Gently place 4 of the crab cakes in the pan and sear for 3 to 4 minutes or until golden brown. Gently turn the cakes over and sear the other side until golden brown. Place them on a baking sheet and into the oven to keep warm. Wipe the pan, add the remaining olive oil and repeat this process for the other 4 crab cakes.

Beer Bread
Marina Variety Store Restaurant
17 Lockwood Dr., Charleston

4 ½ cans beer (your choice)
3 C. sugar
4 oz. honey
1 oz. vanilla

3 oz. butter, melted
8 C. self-rising flour
honey butter

1. Mix first 4 ingredients and let rest for 15 minutes.

2. Slowly incorporate flour and butter until well blended.

3. Pour into 3 greased bread loaf pans.

4. Cook in convection oven at 350°F for 50 minutes. Conventional oven times may vary.

5. Serve warm with honey butter.

Fried Chicken
Martha Lou's Kitchen
1068 Morrison Dr., Charleston

peanut oil, for frying
4 C. flour
kosher salt and freshly ground black pepper, to taste
2 3–4 lb. whole chickens, cut into quarters
2 C. milk
2 eggs

1. Pour oil into an 8-qt. Dutch oven to a depth of 3″, and heat over medium-high heat until a deep-fry thermometer reads 325°.

2. Place flour in a large bowl, season with salt and pepper, and set aside. Season chicken all over with salt and pepper. Whisk milk and eggs in a large bowl, and, working in batches, dip chicken quarters in milk mixture, then dredge in flour, shaking off excess.

3. Place in oil and fry, turning occasionally, until chicken is cooked through and dark brown, 15 minutes for white meat, 20 minutes for dark meat. Drain on paper towels and let cool for 5 minutes before serving.

{ *Nov. 16, 1700: America's first public library*
A law passed by the S.C. General Assembly established a
provincial library in Charles Towne and provided for its
governance. This library, located on St Philip's Street,
remained in operation for 14 years. }

Okra Soup
Martha Lou's Kitchen
1068 Morrison Dr., Charleston

2 tbsp. canola oil
3 strips bacon, finely chopped
½ tsp. dried thyme
6 cloves garlic, finely chopped
1 small yellow onion, finely chopped
1 rib celery, finely chopped
1 bay leaf
Kosher salt and freshly ground black pepper, to taste
2 tbsp. tomato paste
1 lb. okra, trimmed and cut into 1″ slices
6 cups chicken stock
1 28-oz. can whole, peeled tomatoes, crushed by hand

1. Heat oil and bacon in a 6-qt. saucepan over medium-high heat; cook, stirring, until fat renders, about 5 minutes.

2. Add thyme, garlic, onion, celery, and bay leaf, season with salt and pepper, and cook, stirring, until soft, about 5 minutes.

3. Stir in tomato paste; cook, stirring, until caramelized, about 2 minutes.

4. Add okra, chicken stock, and tomatoes; bring to a boil, reduce heat to medium-low, and cook, until okra is very tender and soup thickens slightly, about 45 minutes.

Sea Scallops With Fennel and Broccoli Puree
McCrady's
2 Unity Alley, Charleston

For the scallops:
12 large sea scallops
1/4 C. canola oil
to taste salt and pepper
For the sauce:
1 head broccoli, florets and stems separated
2 C. spinach leaves, stemmed
water
1 Tbsp butter
to taste salt and pepper

For the vegetables:
1 bulb fennel, 1/4" dice, blanched
1 tomato peeled, seed, diced 1/4"
1 C. cauliflower, cut into small florets, blanched
1 yellow squash, cut into 1/4" dice, blanched
2 Tbsp butter to taste salt and pepper
ingredients for the garnish
1 bunch scallion, cut into fine julienne
2 Tbsp white truffle oil

1. Set oven to 300°F.

2. In boiling salted water, cook broccoli stems until very soft, add florets to water and cook until soft as well.

3. When both are soft add the spinach, remove all broccoli and spinach and shock in ice water.

4. Next place the broccoli in blender with spinach and water, puree until smooth.

5. Strain through a fine mesh strainer.

6. To put together the dish in a large sauté pan over high heat, add 1/4 C canola oil.

7. Season scallops with salt and pepper on both sides, add to pan and place in oven.

8. After about 2 minutes turn scallops and cook for about 3 more minutes, remove from the oven and drain the scallops well. Set aside and keep warm.

9. In a medium sauté pan over medium heat, add the butter, then add the fennel, tomato, cauliflower, yellow squash, and season with salt and pepper.

10. Cook until just warm through. Set aside and keep warm.

11. In a small saucepan over low heat add broccoli puree, butter, and water. Heat until just warm. Season with salt and pepper.

12. Place broccoli puree in the middle of the plate, next add the vegetables, and place the scallops atop the vegetables. Garnish with scallions and truffle oil.

Some Charleston Firsts...
1707: America's first woman artist
America's first recognized woman artist, Charles Towne's own Henrietta Johnson, began painting portraits.
Feb. 18, 1735: First opera performed
Colley Cibber's ballad opera Flora, or Hob in the Well, was performed at the Courtroom in Charles Towne.
1780: First Prescription Drug Store
The first prescription drug store began operation in Charles Towne.
July 30, 1774: First business publication
The earliest known edition of South-Carolina Price-Current listed prices for 168 things bought and sold in Charles Towne.
1802: First tea planted
French botanist Francois Andre Michaux (1770-1855) planted tea at Middleton Barony (now known as Middleton Place) near Charleston.

Seared Local Wreckfish with Cauliflower Puree

Middleton Place

4300 Ashley River Rd., Charleston

For Wreckfish:
4 5-6 oz wreckfish filets
2 Tbsp extra virgin olive oil
kosher or coarse ground sea salt, to taste
freshly ground white pepper, to taste
For Cauliflower Puree:
1 Tbsp blended vegetable oil

1 large julienned yellow onion
1 Tbsp minced garlic
1 head of cauliflower; stem removed
1-1 ½ qt heavy cream
4 pats butter
salt & pepper, to taste

1. Place a medium sized, non-stick pan on a medium-high flame. Add the olive oil and allow the pan to heat. Tilt the pan to ensure that the oil coats the surface of the pan.

2. Lightly season the fish with salt and white pepper. Once the pan is hot, gently place the fish flesh side down and sear for approximately 1-2 minutes or until a golden brown sear has been achieved.

3. Once seared, turn the fish over with tongs or a spatula and place in a 375° oven for approximately 8-10 minutes. Pull out of oven and allow to rest until ready to serve.

4. Sweat the onion and garlic in a sauce pot with olive oil.

5. Break apart the head of cauliflower, rinse well and place in a 4 quart pot.

6. Cover the cauliflower with heavy cream and let simmer on low heat for 30 minutes or until the cauliflower begins to soften.

7. Slowly add your butter and begin to blend on a high setting with your immersion blender.

8. When the liquid and cauliflower are incorporated to a smooth silky texture, add your salt and white pepper and serve.

The coiled Sweetgrass basket is an African art that was brought to America by enslaved Africans from the Windward and Rice Coasts of West Africa in the 17th century.

Benne Wafers
Olde Colony Bakery
519 Wando Ln., Mount Pleasant

¾ C. butter
1½ C. brown sugar
2 eggs
1½ C. flour

½ C. sesame (benne) seeds
1 tsp vanilla
¼ tsp baking powder

1. Cream butter and sugar together and mix with other ingredients in the order given.

2. Drop with a teaspoon onto a well-greased cookie pan, far enough apart to allow spreading while baking. They will cook to be a little larger than a quarter.

3. Bake in a 325°F oven for 7 – 10 minutes. (Yield: 7 dozen)

{
Benne Wafers have been a Lowcountry favorite in the Charleston area for over a hundred years. West African slaves introduced sesame seeds to America, and the Nigerian name for them, "benne," stuck in the South Carolina Lowcountry. These wafers are made for classic Charleston recipes and can also be found in many candy shops and stands downtown in the Market.
}

Pimento Cheese
Page's Okra Grill
302 Coleman Blvd., Mount Pleasant

10 lb. sharp Cheddar cheese, shredded
4 C. fresh red pimentos, pickled, and juice
5 lb. pepper jack cheese, shredded
2 C. pickled jalapenos, diced
1 gal. Duke's mayonnaise

3 lb. cream cheese, softened
¼ C. kosher salt
¼ C. black pepper, finely ground
¼ C. granulated garlic

1. In a large mixing bowl, combine the sharp and pepper jack cheeses by hand, tossing well to blend.

2. Add the pimentos and pickled jalapenos and toss.

3. In a separate bowl, mix the mayonnaise and cream cheese until well blended.

4. Combine the spices together and add to the cheese mixture, tossing to evenly coat.

5. Fold the mayo-cream cheese mixture into the cheese mixture, taking care to not overmix and break down the cheese.

6. Refrigerate for several hours or overnight to allow the flavors to meld.

2. Serve with crackers, top on a burger, or a Page's Okra Grill specialty, the P.B.T: pimento cheese, applewood bacon and fried green tomatoes on grilled Texas toast!

Pearlz Rockefellar
Pearlz
Downtown and West Ashley, Charleston

1/4 lb bacon, sliced
1/8 C. shallots, minced
2 Tbsp garlic, minced
1/8 C. celery, diced
1/8 C. onion, diced
1/8 C. white wine
6 oz oyster liquor
6 oz heavy cream
6 oz half & half
1/8 C. basil, lightly packed
1/4 lb baby spinach, half chopped

3 oz crab claw meat
3 oz crawfish tails
2 Tbsp blackening seasoning
1 Tbsp old bay
1 Tbsp ground pepper
3 oz parmesan cheese
4 oz roux

Ingredients for Roux
3 oz butter
3 oz flour

For Roux:

1. To make the roux, mix in equal parts of 3 oz butter to 3 oz flour.

For Pearlz Rockefellar:

1. First render the bacon down and discard 1/2 the bacon fat, or save it and use it for something else.

2. Then add your vegetables and sweat with the bacon until translucent.

3. Next, add your liquid ingredients and bring to a boil. Reduce heat to a simmer.

4. Add your seasoning, crab and crawfish meat.

5. Add your basil and spinach and let that wilt down but not turn brown.

6. Last, add your roux and parmesan and let thicken. Then take off the heat.

For The Rocks

1. To make the topping for the rocks, use half a pound of parmesan and 1 1/2 cup, of bread crumbs.

Iron Skillet Mussels
Peninsula Grill
112 N Market St., Charleston

1 oz olive oil
1 lb mussels
2 oz country ham, julienne
1 oz garlic
2 oz shallots

2 oz white wine
1 oz collard greens
2 oz tomato comcasse
1 oz fresh herb mix

1. Heat a medium sauté pan over medium high heat.

2. Add olive oil, mussels, ham, garlic and shallots. Toss well.

3. Add white wine, collards, tomato concasse and herbs.

4. Cover with second sauté pan or lid.

5. Simmer 2 to 3 minutes.

6. Serve immediately.

The Black Cat Burger
Poe's Tavern
2210 Middle St, Sullivan's Island

Edgar's Drunken Chili:
1 lb ground beef, browned & drained
1 each green & yellow bell pepper, diced
1 yellow onion, diced
1 can stewed tomatoes
2 cans black beans, drained & rinsed
1 Yuengling beer
2 Tbsp garlic, chopped
chili powder, paprika, cumin, cayenne,
black pepper & salt to taste

Home Made Pimento Cheese:
4 oz. cheddar cheese, shredded
4 oz. Monterey jack cheese, shredded
4 oz. ricotta cheese
2 oz. mayo
2 oz. green onions, chopped
3 oz. roasted red bell peppers, pureed
salt & pepper to taste

The Burger:

1. Start by grilling 8 oz. of freshly ground 70/30 chuck to your liking. Serve on a freshly baked bun with lettuce, tomato and pickles. Top with 2 slices of apple wood smoked bacon, grilled onions, Edgar's Drunken Chili and Home Made Pimento Cheese.

Edgar's Drunken Chili:

1. Brown the ground beef in a large pot. Remove from heat, strain grease and hold beef to the side.

2. Sweat the onions and peppers with the garlic until translucent. Add the beef, beans, tomatoes, beer and spices.

3. Bring to a low slow simmer for 45 minutes.

Home Made Pimento Cheese:

1. Combine all ingredients in a bowl and mix. For looser consistency add more ricotta; for thicker consistency use less ricotta cheese.

Much like his work, the life of Edgar Allan Poe was short, tragic and shrouded in mystery. Best known as the author of the popular poem "The Raven", Poe is credited with creating the detective and horror story genres. After a brief stint at the University of Virginia, Poe enlisted in the army under the pseudonym Edgar Allan Perry and was stationed at Fort Moultrie at the western end of Sullivan's Island for thirteen months beginning November 18, 1827. His time on the island inspired "The Gold Bug", a story about a mystical beetle that led to buried treasure.

Fried Green Benedict

Poogan's Porch

72 Queen St., Charleston

For Poached Eggs:
1 gallon water
1 C. oil
1 C. white or rice wine vinegar
4 whole eggs

For Hollandaise Sauce:
3 egg yolks
1 Tbsp cream
1 C. (½ lb) melted butter, cooled to room temperature
1 Tbsp lemon juice or white vinegar
½ tsp salt
1 dash cayenne pepper

1 green tomato
1 whole egg
1 C. whole milk
2 C. flour
2 Tbsp cajun seasoning
1 Tbsp salt
1 Tbsp pepper
2 C. peanut oil

For Buttermilk Biscuits:
5 lb self rising flour
1 C. sugar
½ C. baking powder
1 lb shortening
½ gallon buttermilk

For Poached Eggs:

1. Place water in pot. Add oil & vinegar. Bring to a boil and reduce heat to a simmer, so that a few bubbles break the surface every minute or so.

2. Crack eggs into separate bowls. If the yolk breaks, get a new egg. The yolk needs to be whole.

3. Gently place eggs in the hot water. Cook to desired doneness.

For Hollandaise Sauce:

1. Use a small, thick ceramic bowl set in a heavy-bottomed pan.

2. Off the heat, put the egg yolks and cream in the bowl and stir with a wire whisk until well blended. The mixture should never be beaten, but rather stirred evenly, vigorously, and continuously.

3. Place the container over hot water. If you are setting the bowl in water, there should be about 1½" of water in the pan.

4. Stirring eggs continuously, bring the water slowly to a simmer. Do not let it boil. Stir, incorporating the entire mixture so there is no film at the bottom.

5. When the eggs have thickened to consistency of very heavy cream, begin to add the cooled melted butter with one hand, stirring vigorously with the other. Pour extremely slow so that each addition is blended into the egg mixture before more is added.

6. When all the butter has been added, add the lemon or vinegar a drop at a time and immediately remove from heat. Add salt and a mere dash of cayenne.

For Buttermilk Biscuits:

1. Combine first 3 ingredients and mix well. Add shortening and mix well with hands until shortening is broken up into quarter sized pieces. Add buttermilk and mix until all is incorporated.

2. Roll out to ¾" thickness and cut with biscuit cutter. Place on parchment covered sheet pans ½" apart. Bake at 350° until golden brown.

To Plate Fried Green Benedict:

1. Split a biscuit in half.Put a slice of fried green tomato on each half.

3. Take a small spoon and press it lightly into the tomato to make a slight indention (this will make it easier for the egg to stay on).

4. Add your poached egg into afore mentioned pocket. Add hollandaise sauce to taste.

Steamed Clams in Red Chile Broth

Red Drum

803 Coleman Blvd., Mount Pleasant

4 Tbsp Red Fresno peppers, seeded and diced
4 Tbsp diced Red onion
2 cloves Garlic, finely minced
1 C. dry white wine
6 Tbsp Butter

80 count littleneck clams, scrubbed and soaked in salted water for 1/2 hour to clean
3 tsp guajillo powder
1/2 bunch chopped cilantro leaves

Guajillo powder:

1. Take 6 dried whole guajillo chile pods and toast in 325°F oven for 20 seconds until fragrant. Be careful not to burn chiles.

2. Grind chiles in spice grinder or coffee bean grinder into a fine powder. Store in a airtight container.

Clams:

1. Sweat the onions and peppers over medium heat, 2-3 minutes

2. Add the garlic, white wine and clams, bringing to high simmer

3. Cover and steam 8-10 min approx minutes, or until all the clams are opened.

4. Ladle off clams, and reduce the remaining broth by half.

5. Add butter, Guajillo powder and cilantro, stirring to thicken.

6. Add clams back and serve with grilled french bread

> *Local legend says that Charleston Green, a green so deep it looks black, came about after the Civil War when Union troops sent buckets of black paint to help rebuild the decimated town. Colorful Charleston residents couldn't bear the thought of their Holy City being painted government-issued black, so they tinted the paint with yellow and green, creating Charleston's signature greenish-black accent color.*

> *Isle of Palms was once called Hunting Island nearly 25,000 years ago. And it actually went through another name change. Before being called Isle of Palms, the island that sits to the southeast of Mount Pleasant and the east of downtown Charleston was called Long Island.*

Blackened Tuna Nachos with Watermelon Pico De Gallo

Rita's Seaside Grille
2 Center St., Folly Beach

Tortilla chips
Prepared queso cheese sauce
4 oz. fresh tuna, diced
1 bell pepper, julienned
1 yellow onion, julienned
¼ C. cooked black beans
1 jalapeno, sliced

2 Tbsp cilantro, chopped
6 oz. Monterey jack cheese, shredded
Pico De Gallo:
1 C. watermelon, diced
¼ C. red onion, diced
1 lime, juiced
1 tsp Cajun seasoning

Nachos:

1. Sauté peppers, onions, jalapenos and black beans.

2. Toss tuna with Cajun seasoning and add to pan.

3. Arrange chips on sheet pan, cover with queso cheese sauce and ingredients from the pan.

4. Cover with shredded jack cheese and ½ of the cilantro.

5. Place under broiler until melted.

Pico De Gallo:

1. Combine watermelon, red onion, remaining cilantro and lime juice.

2. Place on top of nachos before serving.

{
African slaves in the Lowcountry created a language and culture they called Gullah. The word may have come from the Gola or Gora Tribes in Angola. The language was made official in 1939 and is creole-based with English as its main base.
"Tek'e foot een 'e han"= to run, or to leave quickly.
"Dry 'long so " = without a reason or explanation.
"Two -time-one-gun"= a double barreled gun.
"Tas'e 'e mout'"= something appetizing to eat.
"Lawfully lady"= lawfully wedded wife.
"Haa'dly'kin"= barely able.
}

Shrimp Creole
SeeWee Restaurant
4808 N Hwy 17, Awendaw

1 55 oz. can whole tomatoes, crushed
1 55 oz. can tomato puree
1 55 oz. can water
8 bell peppers, chopped
6 onions, chopped

1 oz. Old Bay
Salt to taste
3 oz. fresh garlic, chopped
3 lbs shrimp, peeled & deveined

1. Place the whole tomatoes over medium/medium-high heat and boil until tender.

2. Add the tomato puree, water, peppers and onions and reduce heat to simmer for 30 minutes.

3. Add Old Bay, garlic and salt to taste. Cook an additional 30 minutes.

4. Add shrimp and cook 10-15 more minutes, or until shrimp are pink.

5. Serve over fluffy, hot rice.

Oyster Stew in Scallop Cream
Slightly North of Broad
192 East Bay St., Charleston

For Scallop Cream:
4 shallots, rinsed & sliced
1 lb scallops
1 Tbsp butter
2 C. white wine
2 C. heavy cream
1 pinch salt

For Oyster Stew:
1 large Yukon gold potato, peeled & diced medium
1 large leek (light green/white), sliced
¼ lb apple smoked bacon, small dice
1 pint shucked oysters
½ C. chives, chopped
1 tsp butter
1 C. water
1 pinch salt

For Scallop Cream:

1. In a sauté pan, sweat the shallots over medium heat with butter and salt until golden brown, sticky, and caramelized.
2. Deglaze with 2 cups of white wine.
3. Reduce until sticky again. Add cream.
4. Simmer slowly for 15-20 minutes.
5. Strain and discard the scallops.
6. Reserve the cream.

For Oyster Stew:

1. Render the bacon gently for 2 minutes over medium high heat.
2. Discard rendered fat, and save lardons of bacon. Set aside.
3. Cut the leek in half lengthwise and soak in cold water to remove dirt from layers.
4. Once cleaned, slice to form semi-circles.
5. In a medium saucepan, sweat one cup of the sliced leeks in a teaspoon of butter and a pinch of salt over medium heat.
6. Add the potatoes and cook until sticky.
7. Add water, cook until tender, and set aside off heat.
8. In a sauté pan, return the scallop cream to medium heat.
9. Add potatoes, leeks, and bacon.
10. Cook until bubbly.
11. Reduce heat to medium low, add oysters, and heat gently until oysters just crinkle.
12. Add chives, then salt and pepper to taste. Serve.

> *Charleston's first public market was established in 1692 at the corner of Broad and Meeting streets, although a formal brick building wasn't built at the site until 1739. Initially known as the Centre Market, Charleston's City Market was developed as a replacement for the city's Beef Market building, which burned in 1796. In fact, buzzards, also known as "Charleston's Eagles", once trolled the market for meat scraps and kept the place clean and were protected by law.*

Smoked Beef Short Ribs Au Jus
Southend Brewery
161 East Bay Street, Charleston

For Smoked Beef Short Ribs Au Jus
3-4 lbs bone-in Short Rib
½ lb smoked Bacon, small diced
2 cups Carrots, rough cut
3 cups Yellow Spanish Onion, rough cut
2 cups Celery, rough cut
2 qts Beef Stock (fresh or college inn)
3 cups Red Wine (spicy and dry)
¼ cup Worcestershire Sauce
1 tbsp Corn Starch
¼ cup warm Water
2 cups julienne Yellow Spanish Onion

¼ cup of Extra Virgin Olive Oil
1 sprig of Sage
your favorite Vegetable
4 cups Mashed Potatoes

Ingredients for Rub
2 tbsp Kosher Salt
2 tsp Garlic Powder
1 tsp Onion Powder
1 tsp crushed Red Pepper
1 tsp butcher ground Black Pepper
2 tsp Chili Powder

Method for Smoked Beef Short Ribs Au Jus

• Using a smoker or grill heat it to 250°. If you are not using a smoker buy some chips for your grill. If it is a gas grill you will need a chip box to hold your chips. You are only trying to smoke the short rib. If you are using a gas or charcoal grill watch your temperature. You may need to cook the short rib for a shorter amount of time. Remember you want to try and achieve an indirect heat. Note: You may want to put your briquettes on half of your grill using the other half for your short rib. Same for a gas grill light only half.

• While your smoker or grill heats, combine all rub ingredients together.

• Rub all sides of the short rib with the rub mixture. Set aside in your fridge.

• Place your short rib in the smoker or grill and cook for 1-1 1/2 hours. This will not cook the meat all the way but it will give a great flavor for your short rib and sauce. • You will want to turn the beef short rib periodically.

• While your short rib is cooking, get started on the rest of your mise en place.

• Render the bacon in a skillet by cooking it slowly until it is crispy and brown.

• With a strainer, separate the bacon from the fat to stop the cooking process and set aside for later.

• Heat the olive oil in a skillet until hot.

• Place the onions in and cook until caramelized on medium heat. Set aside for later.

• Pull the beef short rib out of the smoker.

• In a roasting pan, place your short rib, wine, rough cut onions, carrots, celery, beef stock, bacon and bacon fat, Worcestershire, and sage.

• Cover the roasting pan with foil and place in the oven for about 2 hours at 300°.

• During the cooking time you will want to turn the beef short rib periodically. At the 1 ½ hour mark cut a small piece to test for tenderness. You will want the short rib to be tender but not falling apart.

• When the beef short rib is ready, take it out and set on a cutting board.

• With a fine strainer pour your au jus into a sauce pot.

• Discard your vegetables.

• At this time, use a knife to cut away the meat from the bone.

• Discard the bone and set the short rib back into the roasting pan. Cover it with foil.

• Cook the au jus down by half on medium heat.

• When the au jus is ready, add your caramelized onions and bring back to a simmer.

• Mix the warm water and corn starch together until smooth.

• When smooth, whisk in the corn starch mixture and cook for 5 minutes at low heat. (Only add the corn starch mixture when the sauce is simmering.)

• Pour the au jus over the short rib. • Place the roasting pan back into the oven at 350° for about 5 minutes.

Peach Crème Brulee
Swamp Fox Restaurant & Bar
Charleston, South Carolina

100 C. heavy cream
65 vanilla beans
275 egg yolks

16-2/3 C. white sugar
2 C and 1 Tbsp white sugar
32 oz fresh peaches

1. In a medium heavy-bottomed pan, heat cream with vanilla beans until bubbles begin to form at edges.

2. Remove from heat and let stand 30 minutes.

3. Beat egg yolks with sugar until pale and thick. Remove vanilla beans from cream and pour into egg yolk mixture.

4. Cook, without boiling, over low heat until mixture thickens and coats the back of a metal spoon.

5. Remove from heat and divide evenly among 6 large ramekins with fresh sliced peaches layered in the bottom.

6. Cover and refrigerate 3 hours, until set.

7. Prior to serving, sprinkle remaining sugar evenly over custards and brown with a kitchen torch or under the oven broiler.

8. Refrigerate until serving.

9. Serve with a slice of fresh peach and a dollop of shantilly cream (optional).

Obviously, this is a recipe used for wedding receptions!

Crab Cakes
The Boathouse at Breach Inlet
101 Palm Blvd, Isle of Palms

1 lb claw meat
1 lb lump meat
1 lb backfin or special meat
2 C. mayonnaise (Dukes)
2 tsp Old Bay Seasoning
2 Tbsp dried parsley
1 lemon, juiced

2 eggs
1 tsp each salt and pepper
3 C. Japanese bread crumbs or Panko
(2 C. for the mixture and 1 C. for the breading)
4 tsp canola or vegetable oil

1. Thoroughly pick the crab meat to remove any hard parts. In a bowl, combine the mayonnaise, old Bay, parsley, lemon juice, eggs, salt and pepper, and wisk until smooth. Add the crabmeat and gently mix in the 2 cups of breadcrumbs and refrigerate for 30 minutes. This gives the bread crumbs time to absorb.

2. From the crab cake mixture into 4 oz or ½ cup cakes. Roll cakes in reserved 1 cup of bread crumbs.

3. To cook the cakes, heat the oil over medium heat in cast iron or fry pan. Place cakes into pan and sear until golden brown; turn over repeat on other side.

Asian Noodles
The Co-Op
2019 Middle St., Sullivans Island

1 lb spaghetti noodles
4 Tbsp sesame oil
4 Tbsp soy sauce
1 tsp sugar
1 tsp balsamic vinegar

½ tsp red pepper flakes
½ C. shredded carrots
½ C. green onions (tops included)

1. Cook spaghetti noodles according to the directions on the package.

2. Place sesame oil in large bowl.

3. Once noodles are cooked, drain well and then place into the bowl with sesame oil. Stir and then add the sugar, soy sauce, balsamic vinegar and red pepper flakes. Mix well.

4. Add the shredded carrots and green onions. Stir again.

5. It's ready to serve! And it's good hot or cold.

Red Pepper Jelly
The Early Bird Diner
1644 Savannah Hwy, Charleston

1 ½ C. sugar
¾ C. pepper vinegar
½ C. pineapple juice
6 red bell peppers, roasted, peeled and chopped

1 jalapeno, chopped with seeds
2 Tbsp pectin
¼ C. diced bell pepper (red or yellow), frozen

1. Combine the sugar, vinegar, pineapple juice, roasted bell peppers and jalapeno. Blend using a food processor or immersion blender.

2. Place the puree in a 2-quart saucepan and bring to a rolling boil.

3. Add the pectin and continue to boil for 60 seconds, at which point add the frozen peppers to stop the cooking process.

4. Pour the jelly into a metal container and chill in an ice bath for about 1 hour until it sets, or overnight in the refrigerator.

Smoked Lamb Ribs
The Grocery
4 Cannon St., Charleston

4 to 5 racks of lamb ribs (8 bones each)
3 Tbsp honey
Spice Mix:
3 Tbsp chili powder

3 Tbsp onion powder
3 Tbsp garlic powder
3 Tbsp black pepper
3 Tbsp kosher salt

1. Season ribs liberally with spice mixture.

2. Prepare smoker.

3. Smoke ribs at 225° for about 2 to 2 ½ hours. Meat should be tender but not completely falling apart.

4. Remove ribs from smoker. You can go directly to the grill or this can be done to this point in advance.

5. Prepare hot grill.

6. Drizzle ribs with honey.

7. Sear on grill until charred.

8. Cut between bones, pile on platter and enjoy.

Barbecued Shrimp with Sautéed Greens

The Ordinary

544 King St., Charleston

Shrimp:
1 C. Worcestershire sauce
¼ C. fresh lemon juice
2 Tbsp hot sauce
10 medium garlic cloves, finely chopped
1 Tbsp finely chopped fresh rosemary
2 tsp kosher salt
3 sticks unsalted butter
1¼ lb 21- or 25-count shell-on shrimp

Greens:
1 Tbsp extra-virgin olive oil
2 garlic cloves, very thinly sliced
¼ tsp dried red pepper flakes
12 C. roughly chopped hardy greens (such as collards, kale or spinach), tough stems removed
½ tsp kosher salt

Poaching the Shrimp:

2. In a medium saucepan set over medium heat, add the Worcestershire sauce, lemon juice, hot sauce, garlic, rosemary and salt.

3. Bring the mixture to a gentle simmer and cook until the sauce is reduced by half and begins to thicken, about 15 minutes.

4. Add the butter, 1 tablespoon at a time, whisking constantly until each piece is melted and the sauce begins to thicken.

5. Reduce the heat to medium-low so that the liquid is barely simmering. Add the shrimp to the sauce and cook until the shrimp are just cooked through, about 5 minutes.

Cook the greens:

1. In a large skillet set over medium-high heat, add the olive oil, garlic and red pepper flakes.

2. Cook, stirring often, until the garlic is fragrant, 30 seconds to 1 minute.

3. Add half of the greens to the skillet and use tongs to turn the greens until they start to wilt, 1½ to 2 minutes.

4. Add the remaining greens and continue to occasionally turn the greens until they have all wilted, about 2 minutes more.

5. Turn off the heat and sprinkle with the salt.

6. Divide the greens among 4 plates and top each with some shrimp. Serve with a small bowl on the side for the shrimp shells.

{ *As the story goes, a ship's log was once discovered that clearly showed a supply of golf balls and clubs had arrived in South Carolina from Scotland sometime in the 1740s. The United States Golf Association agrees that the first golf club to be established in America was the South Carolina Golf Club, which organized in Charleston in 1786 and whose members played some form of golf in a public park called Harleston Green* }

Fried Hominy
The Wreck of Richard and Charlene
106 Haddrell St., Mount Pleasant

1 C. Jim Dandy instant grits
water for grits
salt to taste
2 slices cooked bacon, diced fine
¼ C. pickled jalapenos, diced fine
peanut oil for frying

Dusting powder:
¼ C. all-purpose flour
1 Tbsp garlic powder
1 Tbsp onion powder
¼ tsp cayenne powder
1 tsp salt

Dusting Powder

1. Mix all the ingredients and grind in a coffee grinder until superfine.

Hominy:

1. Prepare the grits per the directions on the box.
2. Continue cooking grits until very stiff.
3. Mix in bacon and jalapenos
4. Pour grits mixture into a 9"x 9" pan, and smooth even, about 1" thick.
5. Refrigerate until the mixture is very firm, about 2-3 hours, or overnight.
6. Spread the dusting powder on a clean surface, and turn out the grits loaf onto it.
7. Cut the loaf into 1" cubes, and lightly dust with the powder
8. Fry immediately in peanut oil at 350°F until golden brown, 3-4 minutes
9. Drain onto paper towels and serve immediately.

Orange & Raspberry Marinated Beets
Tomato Shed Café at Stono Market
842 Main Rd., Johns Island

6-8 medium fresh, whole beets
1/3 C. shallots, finely chopped
1/3 C. raspberry vinegar
½ C. fresh squeezed orange juice
2 tsp extra virgin olive oil

1 large pinch kosher salt
1 large pinch black pepper
2 navel oranges
2-4 C. baby arugula (may substitute for mixed salad greens)

1. Clean the beets and trim off tops leaving about an inch, so the beets don't bleed out while cooking.
2. Boil beets over high heat approximately 1 to 1 ½ hours or until soft (check with knife if needed).
3. Remove beets from heat, strain and let cool.
4. Using a rag, rub beet peel to remove (you may want to wear gloves).
5. After skins are removed cut beets into cubes.
6. Add shallots, raspberry vinegar, orange juice, extra virgin olive oil, salt & pepper.
7. While marinating, zest one orange and add to mixture.
8. Peel oranges, cut them into chunks and stir together with all other ingredients.
9. Chill for 15-20 minutes then serve over arugula.

Pickled Shrimp Salad
Two Boroughs Larder
186 Coming St., Charleston

4 lemons, juiced and zested
1 lb. 16/20 wild-caught S.C. shrimp
1 C. rice wine vinegar
2 cloves garlic, minced
1 shallot, minced
4 whole cloves
4 whole star anise
6 C. water
1 C. white wine

1 bay leaf
1 sprig of fresh thyme
1 Asian pear, julienned
1 Golden Delicious apple, julienned
½ Palmetto sweet onion, julienned
1½ C. cooked green butter beans
2 Tbsp extra virgin olive oil
2 Tbsp minced chives
1 Tbsp minced tarragon

1. Zest and juice four lemons into medium-sized mixing bowl.

2. Add rice wine vinegar, garlic, shallots, cloves, and star anise. Let rest in refrigerator, and peel the shrimp.

3. Bring six cups of water with white wine, black peppercorns, bay leaf, and thyme to a boil in a medium pot.

4. When mixture is boiling, blanch peeled and de-veined shrimp for 40 seconds. You are not cooking the shrimp — just setting the color.

5. Remove the shrimp from boiling liquid and immediately submerge them in ice water to stop the cooking.

6. Remove the shrimp from the ice water and slice in half lengthwise.

7. Add cut shrimp to lemon and rice wine vinegar mixture. Let sit at least four hours, but preferably overnight. The acid in the lemon juice and vinegar will finish cooking the shrimp.

8. Bring four cups of seasoned water to a boil in a medium pot and cook butter beans until tender but not mushy.

9. Remove butter beans from water and cool until salad assembly.

10. Thinly julienne the pear, apple, and sweet onion and mix with butter beans, chives, tarragon, olive oil, shrimp, and 3 Tbs. of marinade.

11. Refrigerate for 2-3 hours to allow the flavors to meld, and serve.

Artichoke Dip
Vickery's
1313 Shrimp Boat Ln., Mount Pleasant

2 14 oz cans quartered artichoke hearts
(whole are fine also)
7 oz Hellman's mayonnaise
3 oz shredded parmesan cheese

1/2 tsp granulated garlic
1/2 tsp white pepper
1/2 tsp salt

1. Drain the liquid from the can of artichokes and discard. Squeeze the excess water out of the artichokes. Finely chop them and place into a mixing bowl. Add the remaining ingredients and mix thoroughly.

2. Spoon into an oven safe serving bowl or container and top with some shredded parmesan cheese and bake until warm. Serve with warm pita slices.

Chicken and Dumplings

Virginia's on King

412 King St., Charleston

For the Chicken :
1 whole chicken
1 bag of carrots
2 yellow onions
1 head celery
3 bay leaves
10 peppercorns
3 sprigs thyme
1 bunch tarragon

1/4 stick butter
salt and pepper, to taste

For the Dumplings :
2 tsp baking powder
1/4 tsp baking soda
1 tsp kosher salt
1 oz. cold shorting
4 oz. butter milk
1 C. all-purpose flour

For the chicken :

1. Place the chicken in a pot and cover it with water and half of all the vegetables. Add all of the herbs except for the tarragon into the pot.

2. Bring the mixture to a boil and then reduce it to a simmer. Boil the chicken until it is done and falling off the bone. Slice the remaining vegetables that were not originally placed in the pot.

For the dumplings :

1. Combine all of the ingredients until they form a paste. Roll the paste out on a floured board and cut it into 1 inch squares.

2. When the chicken is done pull it out of the water and separate the meat from the skin and bone. Strain the liquid from the pot the chicken was in and reduce the liquid by half.

3. Add the tarragon, the sliced vegetables, and the dumplings to this liquid. Cook this mixture until the dumplings and vegetables are almost done then add the ¼ stick of butter.

4. Cook this mixture until it becomes creamy. Season it to taste.

5. Add back in the chicken and gently stir. Serve.

The U.S.S. Yorktown, permanently anchored at Patriot's Point in Mount Pleasant, was initially named Bon Homme Richard after Captain John Paul Jones' Bonhomme Richard (note different spelling), in turn named to honor Benjamin Franklin. Renamed, 26 September 1942, in tribute to USS Yorktown (CV-5), lost three months earlier at the Battle of Midway, thus becoming the fourth US warship to bear the name of a town in Virginia, where the climactic battle of the American Revolution was fought in the autumn of 1781.

Seared Sea Scallops
Wentworth Grill
68 Wentworth St., Charleston

Seared Sea Scallops:
3 each u-10 scallops
2 Tbsp extra virgin olive oil
½ C. pancetta fennel confit
1 each slice toasted almond butter
1 each fennel frond
Pancetta Fennel Confit:
2 each fennel bulb

1 C. pancetta, sliced & julienned
1 tsp extra virgin olive oil
ingredients for almond butter
½ C. almonds, toasted & sliced
2 Tbsp parsley, chopped
1 lb butter, softened
1 tsp salt
1 tsp pepper

1. Julienne the fennel bulbs.

2. Heat oil in sauté pan and add pancetta. Sauté pancetta for a moment and then add the fennel. Sauté until fennel is golden brown and pancetta has rendered its fat. Drain excess grease and discard.

3. Toast almonds until golden. Pull from oven and cool to room temperature.

4. Place butter in mixer and add parsley, salt, pepper, and almonds. When totally mixed, remove from mixing bowl and wrap in plastic to form logs.

5. Season scallops with salt and pepper and sear until deep golden brown. • While cooking your scallops, sauté the fennel pancetta confit.

6. When scallops are done place confit on the plate and place scallops on top of confit. Top each scallop with the toasted almond butter. Place fennel frond on top of scallops and serve.

Ricotta Gnocchi
Wild Olive
2867 Maybank Hwy., Johns Island

1 lb goat cheese
1 lb ricotta
6 ½ cups "00" flour

2 small eggs
1 tsp salt
1 tsp pepper

1. In a stand mixer, add the goat cheese, ricotta, flour, eggs, salt and pepper.

2. Slowly increase the speed until the dough comes together. The dough should be sticky to the touch.

3. Place the dough ball on a floured work surface. Portion the large ball into smaller balls as you go.

4. Roll each smaller ball into ropes about 1 ½ inch thick. Place these ropes on a baking sheet with a towel draped over top.

5. Let the dough rest in your refrigerator for at least half an hour.

6. Once cool, take the roped dough out of the refrigerator - just one or two ropes at a time. Cut into small cylinders.

7. Run the cylinders over the gnocchi paddle board with your thumb. This will cause the dumplings to have ridges and will also create a well to cup the pasta sauce.

8. Roll the gnocchi onto another baking sheet and freeze, if not using that day.

9. Once frozen, you can collect all the gnocchi and place them in a freezer bag and store in your freezer for a later date.

CPSIA information can be obtained
at www.ICGtesting.com
Printed in the USA
LVOW13s0422080617
537332LV00005BA/5/P